FEMALE FIGURE SKATING LEGENDS

Oksana Baiul

Nicole Bobek

Ekaterina Gordeeva

Nancy Kerrigan

Michelle Kwan

Tara Lipinski

Katarina Witt

Kristi Yamaguchi

CHELSEA HOUSE PUBLISHERS

FEMALE FIGURE
SKATING LEGENDS

NICOLE BOBEK

Veda Boyd Jones

CHELSEA HOUSE PUBLISHERS
Philadelphia

Produced by Choptank Syndicate, Inc.

Editor and Picture Researcher: Norman L. Macht
Production Coordinator and Editorial Assistant: Mary E. Hull
Design and Production: Lisa Hochstein

CHELSEA HOUSE PUBLISHERS

Editor in Chief: Stephen Reginald
Managing Editor: James Gallagher
Production Manager: Pamela Loos
Art Director: Sara Davis
Photo Editor: Judy L. Hasday
Senior Production Editor: Lisa Chippendale
Publishing Coordinator: James McAvoy
Cover Illustration: Keith Trego

Cover Photos: AP/Wide World Photos

The Chelsea House World Wide Web site address is
http://www.chelseahouse.com

First Printing

1 3 5 7 9 8 6 4 2

Library of Congress Cataloging-in-Publication Data

Jones, Veda Boyd.
    Nicole Bobek / Veda Boyd Jones.
      p.   cm. — (Female figure skating legends)
    Includes bibliographical references and index.
    Summary: A look at the personal life and skating career of the
young woman who became the National Figure Skating Champion in 1995.
      ISBN 0-7910-5029-7 (hc)
      1. Bobek, Nicole, 1977-   —Juvenile literature. 2. Skaters—
United States—Biography—Juvenile literature. [1. Bobek, Nicole, 1977- .
2. Ice skaters. 3. Women—Biography.] I. Title. II. Series.
GV850.B653J65   1998
796.91'2'092—dc21   98-21902
    [b]   CIP
                                                                    AC

CONTENTS

THE TURNAROUND KID

Nicole Bobek shook off a chill as she waited for her turn to take the ice. The skating arena in Providence, Rhode Island, was cold, and although her skating dress gave her the enchanting look of an ice princess, it wasn't warm. She took a deep breath as the previous skater left the ice, then she skated to the center of the rink. She had great hopes for the 1995 U.S. National Figure Skating Championship, and it required her total concentration.

Up to now Nicole's life had been like skating on an old farm pond in the dead of winter. There had been patchy places where the ice was rough, watery areas where the ice was thin, and thick glassy sections where the ice was smooth. She would skate a little way in

Her leg outstretched in her signature spiral, Nicole Bobek sails across the ice at the 1996 Nationals in San Jose, California.

each part, then turn around and head for a different spot.

She had been through eight coaches in eight years before settling down to a training routine to prove to the figure skating world that she was taking her sport seriously. She was eating right, had lost weight, and was sticking to a rigid schedule.

Nicole had always possessed a graceful talent on the ice and a showmanship that captivated audiences. At 17, she showed a maturity and athleticism that had formerly been missing.

Her latest coach, Richard Callaghan of Detroit, had drilled her on the necessary jumps, which were her weakest points. She protested that she wanted to get the audience's attention, make eye contact, and entertain them, not jump, jump, jump. Callaghan was adamant. Strong jumps were necessary to win.

So Nicole practiced her jumps, lifting herself high into the air, twirling, and landing on one foot. She had memorized her programs and was ready to compete.

On the afternoon of February 10, 1995, Nicole skated her 2:40-minute short program along with 15 others in the senior ladies' division. She performed a nearly flawless program of required elements, which was worth one-third of the final score, and at the end of the day had landed in second place. Bobek was behind Tonia Kwiatkowski, who at 23 was the oldest in the competition, but she was ahead of the favored Michelle Kwan of California, who was only 14. Michelle was strong in the jumps and was learning the artistry that gave the sport such grace. She had placed second at the 1994 Nationals, which is what skaters call the U.S. National Figure Skating Championships, and hoped to claim the 1995 gold medal and become the youngest title holder in history.

Nicole was in a positive state of mind going into the long program on Saturday night. In the months before the competition, she had practiced her routine over and over until it was second nature to her. She was ready for the four-minute free skate, which accounted for two-thirds of the final score.

The leader, Tonia Kwiatkowski, fell on a triple flip jump and landed badly on two other jumps. Her scores left room for others to pass her. Nicole went over her program in her mind, concentrating on the speed and movements necessary to land the jumps that had given her trouble.

When her turn came, next to last, Nicole took the ice in a shimmering blue backless dress, her blonde hair in a pulled-back sophisticated style. She smiled at the sold-out crowd as her music from the movie *Dr. Zhivago* resounded from the loudspeakers.

"It just took me away," Nicole later said of her music, and she skated one of the best performances of her life. At the start, she hit her triple Lutz jump and then completed a triple flip–double toe loop combination. In former competitions, once this difficult beginning was over, she had lost her concentration. But that didn't happen this time, even though she touched her hand to the ice to keep her balance on a triple toe loop landing. She told herself to forget about that minor flub and keep going. She cleanly landed two more triple jumps and a double Salchow. The jumps had given her a little trouble, but she'd stayed upright and remained focused.

She sparkled, she twirled, and she soared across the ice. Her long trademark spiral,

Nearly three decades after winning a gold medal at the 1968 Olympics, Peggy Fleming continued to stay active in the skating world by working as a television commentator at skating events.

gliding on one leg with her other leg held in a mid-air split, left the audience gasping. When she finished her program, she bowed to the crowd's thunderous applause and left the ice, patting her heart with her right hand as if she would faint.

"Nicole is spontaneous, charismatic, and loaded with natural talent," said 1968 Olympic gold medalist Peggy Fleming, who was a commentator for the television coverage. "Inconsistency has plagued her in the past, but it didn't tonight."

Nicole's high marks, mostly 5.7s, 5.8s, and 5.9s out of possible 6.0s from the nine judges, let her pass Tonia for first place. The final skater was Michelle Kwan. Although her style was fluid, she bobbled a landing on one jump and fell on a triple Lutz jump. When Michelle's marks were announced, Nicole Bobek was the new national champion. Michelle was second and Tonia ranked third. Nicole was backstage when she learned of her triumph. She cried on her coach's shoulder. "The score can't be right. It can't be right. There must be some mistake," she said and sobbed.

In her post-victory press conference, she confessed, "I was hysterical. I couldn't believe it at first. I said, 'No, no, I made a mistake,'" referring to the bobbled landing.

She gave credit for her new training regimen to her coach of eight months, Richard Callaghan; to her mother; and to Todd Eldredge, the new men's national champion who also skated under Callaghan's guidance at the Detroit Skating Club.

"This goes to show that a lot of hard work and suffering and a lot of pain is definitely worth it," said Nicole, a self-proclaimed free spirit.

EARLY TRAINING

Nicole Bobek was born in Chicago, Illinois, on August 23, 1977. As a youngster she liked gymnastics, swimming, and ballet, but ice skating was her favorite activity.

Her mother, Jana Bobek, had emigrated to the United States in 1968 after the Communist takeover of her native Czechoslovakia, where she had skated in minor ice skating competitions. Nicole's grandmother had also been a figure skater, so it seemed only natural that Nicole would like ice skating, too.

At three-and-a-half years old, Nicole sat impatiently while her mother laced up her skates, then she stood and tried to keep her balance on the thin blades. She slipped and fell, got right back up, and was soon gliding

When she was young, Nicole practiced pointing her leg at the ceiling in a mid-air split. It later became her signature move.

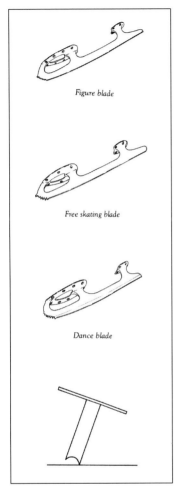

Figure blade

Free skating blade

Dance blade

This illustration shows the different types of skate blades. The figure at the bottom shows the inside and outside edges of a skate blade as well as the groove between them. A skater uses different blade edges to perform each move.

across the rink. She felt freedom as she gained speed and soared on the ice.

Her mother taught her everything she could and enrolled Nicole in a figure skating class sanctioned by the United States Figure Skating Association. The USFSA monitored the levels of skaters who wanted to compete in Olympic-style skating events. Ability to pass proficiency tests, not age, was the criterion for moving from juvenile to intermediate, novice, junior, and ultimately to senior level. Soon Nicole was skating with girls two or three years older, as she passed through the early levels.

When Nicole began skating, the advancement test included compulsory figures. Called school figures, these were a series of circles and complicated patterns on the ice. To master these, Nicole had to learn the basics of skating, including the parts of skate blades.

The blade consists of an inside edge, an outside edge, and a groove between the two edges. The front and back part of the edges allowed Nicole to skate forward and backward. At the front of the skates are teeth, called toe picks, that help a skater jump and spin.

Nicole had to learn to hold an edge, or skate on one edge for a distance. If she skated on the edge long enough, she would curve into a circle. The sharp edge of her skate cut into the ice, leaving a tracing.

The school figures, which Nicole had to learn in order to advance from level to level, were based on two or three linked circles, forming variations on a figure eight. To begin Nicole held an edge on one foot, cutting a circle on the ice. Then she had to skate twice around the same circle, keeping as close to the original tracing as she could. A perfect figure was one in which the circles were no more than a quarter-inch apart.

At test time, USFSA judges measured the distances and determined a skater's proficiency and whether she could move to the next level.

When Nicole started skating, school figures accounted for 30 percent of a skater's total score. The other 70 percent came from the short program, which required certain skating elements, and the longer freestyle program, which allowed a skater to interpret music with spins, jumps, and fancy footwork. This was the part Nicole loved. Even at an early age, she felt the music, moved with it, and slipped her own unique movements into an previously planned program.

One of the first moves her mother taught her was a spiral. Nicole would hold an edge on one foot at a good speed with an exaggerated posed position. She looked like a moving statue on the ice as she held the pose.

Even when she was at home, Nicole's training continued. Her mother made her stand in the living room in a spiral position, posing on one foot, her body leaning forward, her arms outstretched, and her other foot aimed at the ceiling. She learned to hold that position for long seconds and all the while thought of how much she hated that move. Later that lingering spiral became her trademark.

The mandatory figures demanded practice, which Nicole disliked; she preferred dancing across the ice. But her mother was a firm taskmaster, and at six o'clock in the morning Nicole was on the ice, practicing her figures over and over. The tedious routine paid off; she won her first trophy when she was five years old. That same year she had a small part in a Chicago skating production of the *Nutcracker* ballet. Nicole longed to skate the lead as Clara, the little girl who visited the land of enchantment.

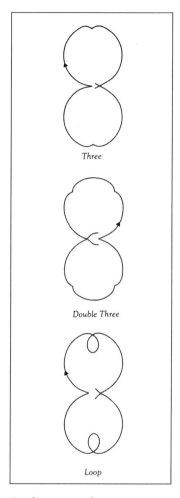

Three

Double Three

Loop

In the compulsory competitions, skaters are judged by the accuracy of the visible tracings their skates leave on the ice. Beginning from a stationary position, a skater must be able to perform any one of the dozens of different school figures, of which three are shown here. Each figure is made with either an inside or outside blade edge.

It was obvious to Jana Bobek that Nicole had talent, and she wanted her daughter to go as far as she could in the sport, with the ultimate goal of winning a world championship and an Olympic medal. Because Jana was a single mother, she struggled for money and time to devote to Nicole's skating. By sharing a house with her friend Joyce Barron, she cut down on living expenses. The two women also went into business together, co-managing ice cream and frozen yogurt trucks in Chicago's Lincoln Park. This job allowed Jana Bobek flexible working hours so she could be with Nicole during her practice times.

Jana Bobek then hired Debbie Stoery as Nicole's private coach. For the next few years Nicole worked with Stoery learning jumps, spins, and spirals. Her energy level seemed limitless as she tackled the difficult jumps.

The differences in the six advanced jumps that were necessary for competitions depended on which inside or outside edge Nicole took off from, which edge she landed on, and if she used the toe pick to vault herself into the air. The easiest jump was the toe loop, followed by the Salchow, flip, loop, Lutz, and the hardest jump of all, the Axel.

The toe loop required the basic rotation position: legs crossed, arms retracted, and head over the left shoulder. She took off from the right back outside edge of her skate, used the left toe pick to vault into the air, made one revolution, and then landed on the same right back outside edge. The jump was simple enough, but she needed two revolutions for a double. When she moved up to advanced levels, she would be expected to make three turns for a triple.

"She was gifted," Stoery said of her pupil. "I loved her to pieces. She was kind and

loving and outgoing." They worked together for four years.

In 1987, when a new mayor was elected in Chicago, Nicole's mother and her partner lost the city park contract. The search for a new job came in second to a search for a new coach for Nicole. They found Barbara Roles Williams, an Olympic bronze medalist, in Los Angeles. Williams, who had won national titles on all three singles levels—novice, junior, and senior— seemed a natural to understand the importance of skating to Nicole.

Jana Bobek took part-time jobs in Los Angeles doing everything from baby-sitting to modeling, so that she could be with Nicole during practice. A rigid school schedule interfered with ice time, so Nicole studied with tutors instead of attending public school.

By the time she was 10, Nicole's skating costs had soared to $20,000 a year. That included

Skaters must learn to exercise power and control in order to perform jumps successfully. Here Nicole falls while attempting to land a jump.

practice sessions on the ice, coaching fees, choreography for her programs, custom-made skates, ballet lessons, skating dresses, USFSA club dues, and travel and medical costs. Money became very tight, but still her mother was determined that Nicole would learn competitive skating.

In 1989 Nicole switched coaches again, to Frank Carroll. Under his direction, she entered novice competition in the Pacific Coast region, where she won third place, which was good enough to send her to novice Nationals, where she placed second.

After these significant wins, renowned coach Carlo Fassi of Colorado Springs called and offered to coach her. Nicole and her mother jumped up and down, crying and laughing. Fassi had coached four Olympic champions, including Peggy Fleming and Dorothy Hamill. This was an opportunity of a lifetime.

Being realistic, Nicole's mother told Fassi that they would need financial help. He promised to find sponsors for her, and he did. When Nicole was 12, they moved to Colorado Springs to train under Fassi. She was on her way to the top.

MOVING AROUND

Life in Colorado was much different from California. Because the USFSA was located in Colorado Springs, the public school system made allowances for the time demands of ice skaters. Nicole enrolled in school and made friends in her classes.

She and Carlo Fassi hit it off wonderfully. They worked well together, and Nicole passed the test to move up to the junior division. Skating costs mounted and practice sessions demanded more time. Attaining junior status was a rung on the ladder toward becoming a senior and the hope of one day making it to the Olympics.

Nicole excelled in the smooth ballet movements that made ice skating so graceful and were important for a good artistic presentation

---

When Nicole Bobek was 12, she performed at the 1990 U.S. Olympic Festival, where George Steinbrenner saw her. Steinbrenner was so impressed with her performance, he helped sponsor her training.

World champion skater Ulrich Salchow, shown here with a young Sonja Henie, invented the Salchow, a jump named in his honor.

score. But jumps were critical in getting good marks in the technical area, so Nicole focused on learning those jumps.

For the Salchow, invented by Ulrich Salchow of Sweden, 10-time world champion in the early 1900s, Nicole took off from the left back inside edge, made a revolution, then landed on the right back outside edge.

The loop jump was like the toe loop, except that Nicole could not use the toe pick to push herself into the air. She started from the right back outside edge, made one revolution, then landed on the same right back outside edge. It was not a difficult jump, but one revolution wasn't good enough. To compete in juniors she would need at least three triple jumps, and this was one of the easier ones to learn.

To help Nicole get the timing right for the triples, she wore a harness. It lifted her up for the jump until she could develop the strength in her legs to get the height required for three rotations.

In 1990 Nicole won the Southwestern junior regional competition and from there went on to National Junior Championships, where she placed fourth. She had trained intensely for both events but came away from the Nationals knowing that she'd have to work harder to place higher the next year.

While Nicole practiced her jumps and skating, the International Skating Union (ISU), of which the USFSA was a national branch, was embroiled in a debate about the importance of school figures in competition. TV viewers were confused by the judging at Olympic figure skating events. A skater could score high in freestyle skating, but not win a medal because of a low score on the boring, rarely televised school figures. In the early 1960s the compulsory figures accounted for 60 percent of a skater's final score, but by 1991 the school figures, from which figure skating got its name, were no longer required in international competition. Televison viewers wanted to watch graceful dancing, jumps, and spins, and they wanted the skater who did this best to win a medal.

Nicole was elated by the news. Even though the figures forced a skater to learn control, they were drudgery. She had always disliked them, and if the coach was looking the other way, she would goof off instead of practicing them. Nicole could practice the edges and turns, formerly learned from the figures, in free-skating exercises. She could free-skate for hours, expressing emotions she felt in the music, and she gloried in it. But she also knew that now those jumps would be more important than ever.

In the summer of 1990, Nicole skated at the U.S. Olympic Festival, an annual event where future Olympic hopefuls in different sports could test their skills against their peers. In the audience was New York Yankees managing partner George Steinbrenner. He was so amazed at the 12-year-old's grace and charismatic style, he wrote a $15,000 check for her training.

Other sponsors helped with the bills, which allowed Nicole to keep working toward her dream of an Olympic medal. She was invited to

Canada's Vern Taylor became the first person to land a triple Axel when he successfully completed three and a half mid-air rotations during the 1978 Worlds in Ottawa.

a USFSA-sponsored elite training camp, where top coaches taught her to skate with style. Her mother had opened a tanning salon, which also helped with the bills. Life seemed to be going smoothly until Carlo Fassi moved to Italy in 1991 to manage an ice rink and coach. The Bobeks followed, but the cost of living abroad was so high and Fassi's coaching time was so limited, they ended up staying only four months before moving back to Colorado Springs.

Nicole began training with Fassi's replacement, Kathy Casey, and life assumed a new kind of normalcy. She was back in public school again with a regimented schedule. By eight o'clock each morning she was in class. At noon she had lunch, then went to the skating rink for one o'clock ice time. Weight training was at 3:00. All those jumps and turns and spirals required great athletic skill; lifting weights built and toned her muscles. She ate supper at 4:30, then skated for another two hours. Then came homework, and sleep, and it was time to start all over again.

The regimen paid off. In 1991 she placed fourth in the World Junior Championships, and in her first Nationals in the senior division, she placed a respectable eighth. She won both the U.S. Olympic Festival and the Vienna Cup.

"Most of my friends get to hang out a lot, but I don't have time," Nicole said. "I don't go to school dances, I can't be in the school play, I can't play soccer, and I've always had to miss gym class."

But there were tradeoffs. Others in her class at school were not flying to Europe or across the United States and Canada for competitions. And after each competition, "there's always another party," Nicole said.

New York Yankees manager George Steinbrenner contributed $15,000 toward the cost of Nicole's training.

Her mother said Nicole had a positive attitude about her time away from Colorado Springs. "If she's upset about missing a big night with her friends because of a skating event, she'll just make sure she has a great time."

Nicole woke up one November day in 1991 crying out in pain. After a diagnosis of appendicitis, Nicole was wheeled into the operating room to have her appendix removed. The operation went well, but she choked from the anesthesia, causing her lungs to collapse. For 24 hours she lay in critical condition, hooked up to machines, fighting for her life.

Nicole recovered and started skating as soon as possible. By January 1992 she was able to place seventh at the Nationals. Then she fell ill with mononucleosis. She was tired and discouraged, and talked of quitting skating. Her mother reminded her that she had a gift from God that she needed to share with others. "If I had thought she really wanted to stop skating," Jana Bobek said, "I would never have forced her to continue. But I noticed that even though she slacked off, she still went to practice. If I gave in when she said, 'I don't want to do it anymore,' she might have been unhappy for the rest of her life. So I didn't let her quit."

The mother-daughter relationship suffered after this, and Nicole behaved like a rebellious teenager. She wanted to spend more time with her friends, hanging out at the mall. She wanted to have dates with boys. She wanted a balanced life, a life outside of skating. But her mother overruled Nicole's feisty personality. Skating practice became more intense as Nicole dropped out of public school and continued her education with tutors.

As her body developed through puberty, she endured sporadic weight gains and added inches in height, widening hips, and a developing bust. All affected her jumping ability. The flip was really a toe-assisted Salchow, not a difficult jump, but it had to be high if she was to get in three revolutions. For a Lutz jump, named after its inventor Alois Lutz, Nicole took off on her left back outside edge with a right toe-pick assist. She revolved counterclockwise and landed on her right back outside edge.

The hardest jump of all was the Axel, named for Axel Paulsen, who performed the jump at the first known international style competition in Vienna in 1882. She had to take off on her left forward outside edge, rotate counterclockwise, and land on her right back outside edge. A triple Axel required three and a half rotations. Few female skaters had landed the triple.

Nicole had not mastered it by the 1993 Nationals, but she skated well enough to place fifth.

Convinced that she was headed upward, Nicole subdued her rebellious nature and concentrated on doing whatever it took to be the best.

MORE CHANGES

The skating season for Olympic-eligible skaters is from fall to early spring. Fall competitions include local or regional qualifying events and invitational trips. The latter, which must be ISU-sanctioned, allow skaters like Nicole to learn nerve-calming techniques when skating in front of crowds. In January or early February, Nationals are held, and the World Championships, called Worlds, are usually in March. The rest of the year is filled with practice and more practice.

Nicole was still struggling with her jumps, but when the 1993–94 season began, she took time off from practice to fly to Paris to compete in Trophy Lalique, where she placed fifth. She placed second in the U.S. Pro-Am Challenge, and looked more like a pro than an

Nicole, who sometimes lacked focus and discipline, had to work hard to improve her performance.

Olympic-eligible skater. Even though she didn't have all the triples, she had a presence that crowds loved. It was an intangible quality, the undefinable "it," that let her sparkle on the ice.

She qualified for 1994 Nationals by placing second in the Southwestern senior competition and headed for Detroit, Michigan, for practice sessions. The Nationals were a qualifying ground for the '94 Olympic team from the United States. The intense competition rated headlines in the media.

Skater Nancy Kerrigan was at the arena for practice one day when a man ran by and clubbed her leg with a police baton. Nancy crumbled. She had been a favorite to win, and now she was out of the competition because of her knee injury. Doctors said that with physical therapy Nancy could be skating again within a couple of weeks.

Tonya Harding won the event, Michelle Kwan came in second, and Nicole earned the bronze medal. As the Nationals champion, Tonya was assured one of the two spots on the Olympic team. Normally the second place winner would have also been named, but that decision was up to the USFSA committee. Nancy Kerrigan appealed for a medical exemption and asked to be named to the team. Because Kerrigan was the 1993 Nationals champion, the committee voted to give her the second spot on the team.

A few days later Tonya Harding came under suspicion as part of the plot to injure her toughest competitor. With no proof against her, the USFSA let her go to the Olympics in Norway.

The Tonya/Nancy rivalry garnered an unprecedented TV audience to watch them skate in the long program in the Olympics. Only three football Super Bowls have had more viewers. The drama whetted America's appetite for figure skating. Television executives took notice and began to air more skating events.

By the 1994 Worlds, Harding had been charged with participating in the planning of the attack on Kerrigan. She paid hefty fines, was sentenced to community service, and was ordered to quit the USFSA and pull out of Worlds.

With Nancy Kerrigan turning pro, that left Michelle Kwan and Nicole Bobek, the second and third-place finishers at the Nationals, to represent the United States at the 1994 Worlds in Japan.

Nicole was unprepared for the event. With only a few days to get in shape, she flew to Japan and skated, but failed to survive the qualifying round for the long program. Despite her lack of preparation she finished 13th in Group B, against the best in the world.

Then suddenly, in the summer of 1995, Nicole's mother said it was time to move on, and a 17-year-old Nicole had her sixth coach. The Bobeks moved to Massachusetts, where Evy and Mary Scotvold operated an ice rink on Cape Cod.

The Scotvolds were strict disciplinarians, who looked unfavorably on Nicole's half-hearted attitude toward her practice. When she wanted to go to the ISU-sanctioned Goodwill Games

At a press conference, skater Nancy Kerrigan describes the attack on her at the 1994 Nationals. After her role in the attack was discovered, skater Tonya Harding was disqualified from the 1994 Worlds and Nicole Bobek was elected to participate in her place.

in Russia to make a few thousand dollars, Evy Scotvold said she should stay home and practice. She went anyway, and coach and skater parted.

Scotvold later said, "She was funny and sweet. We got along really well. . . . She just doesn't have any discipline."

Next stop for Nicole was Detroit and coach Richard Callaghan. By this time she was 10 pounds overweight for a skater and had an odd habit in practice: when skating her program, if she made a mistake, she would stop, and not pick herself up and catch up with her music.

At the beginning of the 1994–95 season, Callaghan took Nicole to Sun Valley, Idaho, to skate in a TV promotion. Five ladies skaters had been invited to the October event, and Michelle Kwan was one of them. Callaghan wanted to see how Nicole measured up against Kwan. There was no contest. Michelle looked polished, while Nicole looked erratic. Michelle came in first; Nicole came in a sloppy second and complained of a bad hip.

The next Olympic-eligible competition was Skate America, held in Pittsburgh. At lunch before the ladies' competition, Nicole ate with her mother and her mother's friend, Joyce

Coach Richard Callaghan, shown here with national champion Todd Eldredge, helped Nicole to get in shape and discipline herself following her disappointing performance at the 1994 Worlds.

Barron. Nicole ordered a Philly cheesesteak sandwich with extra cheese, peppers, and mushrooms. At another table in the restaurant, Michelle Kwan ordered chicken stir-fry.

The old adage—you are what you eat—was true. Michelle skated elegantly. Nicole looked lethargic. While Michelle turned a planned triple jump into a double, Nicole landed no triples at all, fell on a jump, and said she still had a bad hip.

That night before the exhibition skating, Nicole was out late, while Michelle kept early-to-bed training hours. The next day, Michelle skated beautifully, and Nicole crashed to the ice on an easy jump.

It was time for some changes. Nicole realized she had to work and work hard. Richard Callaghan ordered her to eat only salads until she got her weight down. He required four complete run-throughs of her program each day in practice.

Two-time national champ Todd Eldredge was also training with Callaghan. Nicole watched the intensity with which he practiced and followed his example.

Callaghan let her put her personal touch on her choreography—to a point. "I get the idea of what she does, memorize it and teach it back to her," he said. But he stopped her improvising in mid-program when the music or the crowd moved her.

"She was liable to throw in just anything out there," Eldredge said. Now that she was more disciplined, her skating improved. When January and the 1995 Nationals arrived, Nicole was ready. None of her ex-coaches was surprised by her victory in the 1995 Nationals. They all expressed the same opinion. If Nicole developed a work ethic, which now seemed firmly in place, she was unstoppable.

IN THE
PUBLIC EYE

An odd thing happened on the way to the 1995 Worlds in Birmingham, England—Nicole's past caught up with her. Six days after Nicole's victory at the Nationals, the *Detroit Free Press* broke the story of her arrest on a burglary charge.

On November 2, 1994, Nicole had entered a skating friend's home using the electronic security code her friend had given her. Nicole said she went inside to wait for her friend. When the friend's father came home, he allegedly found her with money she had taken from a closet.

Nicole said it was all a misunderstanding, and her lawyer said nothing was taken. Instead of defending against a burglary charge in what would have been a media frenzy, Nicole entered a conditional guilty plea to a charge of home invasion. She was sentenced to two

---

Despite the negative publicity she received prior to the 1995 Worlds, Nicole was able to win the short program with five 5.9s.

years of probation under a law that made the charge confidential and would remove it from her record after probation was completed.

Because the charge became public knowledge, circuit court judge David Breck dismissed the case, and Nicole's record was now clean.

But that didn't stop the stories. The *National Enquirer* put Nicole's picture on the cover with the headline "America's New Skating Champ is a Burglar, The Tragic Untold Story." *People* magazine printed accusations that Jana Bobek and her friend Joyce Barron had mistreated Nicole. The reporter recounted an episode when Nicole had run away for two days when she was 16. Although Nicole admitted that she'd run away to the house of Joyce Barron's grown daughter, she said it was a case of everyone wanting to control her.

Nicole defended her mother. "I would just like to say this. My mother has never hit me."

British tabloids covered the story and printed everything ever known about Nicole. Coach Callaghan admitted that he gave her the nickname "Brass Knuckles" because she liked to wear a ring on every finger and even her thumbs. He stopped that practice, but the nickname had caught on and was used against her in the press.

Nicole kept cool and calm while the papers called her names and sullied her reputation. At the standard press conference before Worlds, she faced a room of English and foreign journalists and read a statement.

"The last two weeks have been very difficult for me. I have grown a lot as a result. All of you are aware of the things that have been brought up in the media. I'd like to say that there is nothing new. Mr. Callaghan and I have been able to put this behind me and focus my efforts on training for the World Championships."

Reporters went along with the press conference rule that no questions were to be asked about the arrest, and Nicole acted as if it had never happened. She was charming, witty, and grinning. She was here to skate, not defend herself to reporters, and skate she did.

The best in the world gathered together and took the ice one by one for the short program. During the 2:40-minute program, skaters had to complete required elements: a double Axel, double jump or a triple jump; a jump combination that can be a double and triple or two triples; a flying spin, layback, or sideways leaning spin; a spin combination with one change of foot and at least two changes of position; one spiral step sequence; and a step sequence of a different nature. The moves could be done in any order, but there were automatic deductions if skaters missed any of the elements.

Nicole skated in a dazzling white dress to Russian folk music. She skated with a swish and a whirl, but took off a little late for her triple Lutz jump. She came down in a strong landing and added a double toe loop for the combination. So far her jumps, always her nemesis, were going fine.

Her spin combination was outstanding and her trademark spiral held the audience spellbound. Next she successfully landed the double Axel and began the layback spin. For this movement, Nicole leaned back with her free leg extended at a 45-degree angle and held her arms out to her sides in a graceful position. With each rotation, Nicole looked at the same fixed point at eye level, so she wouldn't get dizzy, and she concentrated on staying in one spot instead of traveling across the ice. After this crowd-pleaser, she landed a triple toe loop; a flying sit spin completed her short program.

She had skated a clean program, and she was breathless in "kiss and cry," the area where coaches and skaters sit while awaiting their scores. If the scores are good, they kiss; if they are bad, they cry. Sometimes when the scores are good, they cry because it is an emotional time.

Nicole's marks were high, and by the end of the day, no one had scored better.

"I had no idea I might get first place," she said. "Winning the Nationals has left me feeling I can do anything. It has helped me a lot.

"Right now I'm very excited and I'm trying to calm myself down for the free program tomorrow. I'm trying not to be too excited so I can do what I have to do then."

Olga Markova of Russia was in second place, followed by China's Chen Lu, Surya Bonaly of France, and in fifth place, Michelle Kwan, who had skated a flawless program.

Three of Nicole's ex-coaches were at the Worlds: Kathy Casey, Frank Carroll, and Carlo Fassi. No one was surprised by her short program performance.

"When she's on, she's on," Fassi said. "Nicole has a sparkle that's incredible. She's a natural, she's exciting. It's nothing studied. Some have it, some don't. She has it."

With great hopes for a world championship, Nicole skated in the long program on Saturday. In the freestyle skate, she could do any movements she wanted, and the more difficult the moves, the better her technical score. She wore a shimmering blue backless dress and wore her blonde hair pulled back in a French braid. During her first two minutes on the ice, she looked unbeatable. Her style was beautiful and her jumps terrific. She landed a triple Lutz–triple toe loop combination, a triple flip–double toe loop combination, a triple toe loop and a high double Axel.

Then she fell—twice, on a triple loop and a triple Salchow.

After she finished her program, she sat in kiss and cry with her bottom lip trembling and fought back tears. She had almost pulled it off, almost won the Worlds. Those jumps had cost her dearly.

When all had skated, Nicole had won the bronze medal—third place.

"It wasn't my best performance," she admitted. "I was upset I missed those two jumps. But I am pleased I ended up with a medal and pleased with the way I did it."

Figure skating judging is subjective, and there has been a long-standing deference to pecking order—allowing a skater to grow, wait her turn, and come back next year. Appearance

Despite falling on a triple loop jump and a double Axel during her long performance at the 1995 Worlds, Nicole was able to come away with the bronze medal.

was important, and Michelle Kwan, who had skated the best performance of her life to finish fourth, looked like the 14-year-old that she was with her ponytail and minimal makeup.

In contrast, 17-year-old Nicole looked 25, sophisticated, and womanly. That was the look of a figure skater that the judges wanted. Although she'd been held back before because of her attitude and teenage shenanigans, this time Nicole benefited from the judges' bias.

With a national title and a bronze medal from the Worlds, Nicole hired the William Morris Agency to represent her in skating endeavors. She was included in Tom Collins' prestigious Campbell Soup Tour of World Figure Skating

A thrilled Nicole Bobek receives the bronze medal at the 1995 Worlds. On the platform with her are Chinese skater Chen Lu (gold medal) and French skater Surya Bonaly (silver).

Champions that hit the road in the summer. The pay was excellent, and it would help her pay her soaring skating costs.

When the tour went to Chicago, Nicole returned to the McFetridge Sports Complex where she had first skated when she was three. There she spoke to 100 children about skating and life. A week earlier, she had spoken in Maryland to 300 elementary school children as part of her national campaign, "Touching the Heart—Raising the Spirit."

Nicole admitted that she'd grown up during the last few months. Her coach agreed that she'd gone through hard times, but had fought back.

"I think I draw a lot of the media attention because I'm a very open person. It makes me mad when they get stuff wrong, but people will believe what they want to believe anyway. I don't particularly like my image as the bad girl of figure skating, but I don't want to deny my flair either, or lose my individuality.

"My goal now is to win an Olympic medal. I dream of it all the time, of giving the performance of my life. If I accomplish that goal, I'm set up for life. I'll turn pro, I'll have my own ice shows. Once I'm an Olympic champion, everything will be great."

UP AND DOWN SEASONS

Nicole liked being on top. She liked the spotlight and the tour that earned her good money. Now she believed she was ready for the big time. She hired a publicist and a manager, and accepted a fashion shoot for *Vogue* magazine. One skater aptly called her "Marilyn on Ice," referring to movie star Marilyn Monroe's charismatic appeal. Blonde and attractive, Bobek had a tremendous on-ice appeal.

While Nicole was getting her team together, ice skating was becoming a big money venture. *Business Week* magazine surveyed Americans (both men and women) and found that four of their top seven favorite sports were figure skating: 1) football, 2) ladies' figure skating, 3) gymnastics, 4) baseball, 5) pairs figure skating, 6) men's figure skating, 7) ice dancing.

Nicole Bobek and her coach Barbara Roles Williams announce her withdrawal from the 1996 Nationals because of injury.

Made-for-TV skating events appeared on many channels with no shortage of sponsors, and pay for skaters skyrocketed.

For Olympic-eligible skaters, there were fewer opportunities to make money than for those skaters who had already won Olympic medals and had turned pro. Some invitation-only events, like the Hershey's Kisses International Challenge in Los Angeles, were USFSA-approved and allowed skaters like Nicole to earn money. She was invited to compete, and so was Michelle Kwan. At this event, Michelle came out on top. Nicole finished a disappointing fourth. At the Best of the Best, another exhibition-style competition, Nicole came out on top, with Michelle in second place. But there were many events where Nicole could not skate without turning professional, thus becoming ineligible for the Olympics. Olympic officials recognized the lure for skaters to turn pro. They countered it by providing financial incentives of their own.

For the 1995–96 season, they introduced the Champions Series of Figure Skating which boasted nearly $2 million in prize money. Much like the Grand Slam in tennis, the Champions Series would be a five-event international circuit. At each event, the winner would earn $30,000, second place would earn $18,000, third would earn $10,000, plus points for each medal. Skaters would accumulate points at each event, and the six skaters with the most points would skate at the Champions Series Final.

The events that made up the Champions Series were Skate America, Skate Canada, Trophy de France, Nations Cup in Germany (now called Cup on Ice), and NHK Trophy in Japan. A season later a sixth event, Cup of Russia, was added. All the competitions were televised, giving the Olympic-eligible skaters exposure and the opportunity for name recognition.

The first event of the series was Skate America. This competition had been around for 13 years as an international skating exhibition. Now it had more legitimacy, since a gold medal was accompanied by a check that could help to pay a skater's staggering training expenses.

Again, Nicole and Michelle skated head to head. Michelle won the gold and $30,000; Nicole came in sixth. Michelle went to Skate Canada and came home with another first-place check, while Nicole skated in the Starlight Challenge, an exhibition-style competition, and won first place there. At the Nations Cup in Germany, Michelle again took the gold, and Nicole won third and the $10,000 prize money.

Michelle Kwan had accumulated enough points to skate in the Champions Series Final. Nicole had not. But there was still an opportunity to earn big money. The Nutcracker on Ice touring group was looking for a skater to be Clara, the role that Nicole had dreamed about when she was five years old and had played in the Chicago production of that Christmas classic. Pay was a reported $90,000 for a month's work, but the skater would have to perform in 20 cities between Thanksgiving and Christmas.

It was a double deal. National men's champion Todd Eldredge signed on as well, and he and Nicole's coach, Richard Callaghan, went along for afternoon training sessions. Nicole needed the practice. The 1996 Nationals were scheduled for the third week in January. Most skaters were staying focused, skating their short and long programs over and over in December, not memorizing them between play performances.

During the tour Nicole aggravated a tendon injury on her inside right ankle, the ankle she landed on when jumping. Although a doctor recommended that she take a few weeks to rest, Nicole said she had no time to take off. She fulfilled her contract and skated the entire Nutcracker tour.

Along the way she and Richard Callaghan parted ways. Nicole replaced him with Barbara Roles Williams of Las Vegas, who had coached her eight years earlier.

With 1996 Nationals scheduled for January 14–21, Nicole had little time to train with her new coach. Still nursing her ankle injury, Nicole hoped to skip the competition and asked the USFSA for a bye onto the United States team for Worlds. The Nationals champion automatically went to Worlds. Normally the second and third-place finishers were awarded the other two spots, but a committee made that final decision.

The USFSA made no promises and advised Nicole to show up and skate. Nicole traveled to San Jose, California, for the event. She held a breezy press conference and when asked about the differences in her style and that of 15-year-old Michelle Kwan, Nicole said, "I'm a woman."

Practice did not go well. Once again, Nicole was having trouble with her jumps. For the short program of required elements, she skated out in her glittery blue dress and did all right, but she touched her hand to the ice for balance when she landed her triple Lutz–double toe loop combination jump, which knocked her down in the scoring.

At the end of the short competition, it was no surprise that Michelle Kwan was in first place; she had skated consistently all season. Tonia Kwiatkowski was second, and Nicole third.

The next morning Nicole practiced and said her ankle was fine, but in the afternoon it began to swell. That evening Nicole took the ice for warmups with the final group of skaters. Her ankle throbbed when she jumped.

While Michelle was skating a program that included seven triple jumps, Nicole had an orthopedist examine her ankle. The doctor, Nicole, and her coach conferred and all agreed that she should withdraw from the competition. Since their decision was announced before Nicole's turn to skate, 13-year-old Tara Lipinski, who would have followed Nicole, went right onto the ice.

Nicole told reporters she was sad about the decision to withdraw, and then she burst into tears. Meanwhile tiny Tara landed five triple jumps in her program.

Michelle Kwan won the Nationals, followed by Kwiatkowski and Lipinski. Again Nicole and

Italian coach Carlo Fassi, who had coached her when she was young, was Nicole's favorite. In 1996, after Fassi returned to the U.S., Nicole began studying with him once again and worked her way back up to a bronze medal at the 1997 Nationals.

her coach appealed for a bye onto the U.S. team. After all, Nancy Kerrigan had asked for a medical exemption when she, as the reigning Nationals champ, had been unable to skate after the knee incident, and she'd been granted a spot on the 1994 Olympic team.

The USFSA committee took it under consideration and denied Nicole's request. It sent Michelle Kwan, Tonia Kwiatkowski, and Tara Lipinski to the 1996 Worlds instead. Nicole was left at home to rest her ankle. To Nicole and her coach the message from the committee was clear. If a skater practiced and took the USFSA seriously, she would be rewarded. If the lure of money and glamour in exhibition-style skating came first, then a skater would not be taken seriously.

Undaunted, Nicole vowed to come back, despite a back injury that kept her off the ice for several months in 1996. With new resolve, Nicole changed coaches once again. This time she returned to Carlo Fassi, whom she'd always admired, but who had moved to Italy when she was young. Now he was back in the United States, coaching out of Lake Arrowhead, California. The mutual respect they had shared when she was a youngster was still there, and she thrived under his guidance.

Even though she had not entered one major competition in 1997 because of her back and ankle injuries, Nicole was determined to do her best at the 1997 Nationals. Few reporters paid attention to her because they were writing story after story about Michelle Kwan, the reigning champion, and Tara Lipinski, the young whirling dervish. Both girls were jumpers, and the jumps were still Nicole's weakest area in competition.

Nicole did not start off with a bang at the Nationals—she stumbled to sixth place after the short program, but she refused to give up. On Saturday night she glided out on the ice in a Heidi-type costume and skated to music from the ballet *Giselle*. She attempted only four triples, but she landed them cleanly. Her presence on the ice, her dramatic interpretation of the music, and her gracefulness in her movements brought the crowd to its feet in a thunderous standing ovation.

Nicole's smile lit up the place. "I was thinking 'Whoa. Wow! It's a miracle!' I thank God—and a lot of other people," she said after her glorious performance. For the moment she was in first place in the long program.

An emotional Nicole Bobek, whose coach Carlo Fassi died of a heart attack a few days earlier, kneels on the ice after her performance at the 1997 Worlds in Lausanne, Switzerland.

Michelle Kwan skated next and fell apart on the ice. She fell twice and touched her hand down on another jump. The audience gasped. What had happened to the champ?

Next to skate was Tara. She cleanly landed seven triples and skated away with the title. Nicole came in second in the long program. She earned the bronze medal, which guaranteed her another trip to the Worlds. "I wanted to skate great for everyone who has never given up on me," Nicole said.

In the month between the Nationals and Worlds, Nicole worked hard on her jumps. She lifted herself high into the air, whirled, and landed on one foot. She had been given another chance, and she wasn't going to blow it.

But at the 1997 Worlds at Lausanne, Switzerland, tragedy struck. Nicole's coach, Carlo Fassi, suffered a massive heart attack at a practice session. Before he died he told Christa, his wife and coaching partner, "Please be with Nicole for her competition."

Fassi's death hit Nicole hard. She hid her red puffy eyes behind dark glasses as she spoke to reporters, but she couldn't hold back the tears. "He always cared," she said. "He took the place of being a dad. If I was dating, he wanted to know who it was—and he wanted to meet him."

With only three hours sleep, Nicole stepped onto the ice for the short program. Again the jumps gave her trouble, and she stumbled on her triple Lutz and fell on her triple toe loop. Those mistakes landed her in eighth place after the short program.

"My warmup felt great, but right before I did the program, I looked at Christa and began crying," Nicole said. "I know how hard it was on her, but it meant so much to have her with me."

Nicole didn't have the physical stamina in the long program to land the difficult triple jumps. As her music ended, she dropped to her knees in a prayerful pose and buried her head in her hands. The audience mourned with her. "I told Carlo I tried and that I loved him," she later said.

Tara Lipinski earned the gold medal, Michelle Kwan was awarded the silver, and Vanessa Gusmeroli of France received the bronze. Nicole's 13th-place finish wasn't important to her in the face of the tragedy, and she vowed to stick with Christa Fassi as her coach. "She has Carlo in her heart. I know that when I am with her, he is always around."

SPINNING AROUND
AND AROUND

After the devastating Worlds, skating no longer seemed as important to Nicole Bobek. Most figure skaters live for that moment on the ice. Their lives are focused around a skating rink, but Nicole wanted more. She wanted skating to be a part of her life, but not all of it. She wanted a balanced life. Her pursuit of an Olympic medal ruled that out.

In the off-season before the January 1998 Nationals, which would be the Olympic qualifier, Nicole changed agents and moved her permanent residence from Detroit to Jupiter Island, Florida, even though she continued to train at Lake Arrowhead, California. She again skated on the summer tour with the Campbell Soup Tour of World Figure Skating Champions and was a crowd-pleaser as usual, even though

Nicole performs her long program at the 1998 Olympics in Nagano, Japan.

inconsistency plagued her and she often fell on one of her jumps. She sustained ankle and back injuries in one fall.

She finished fifth in Nova Scotia at Skate Canada after falling in both the short and the long programs. A couple of weeks later in the Cup of Russia competition, she finished sixth, landing just one triple and falling on two others. She looked for the silver lining in all her trouble with the jumps. Maybe she could get them over with before the Nationals. She had wanted a chance at an Olympic medal for so long, and now was the time to get her act together and focus on that goal.

Nicole settled down to practice hard and work on her jumps. Media attention focused on the Tara Lipinski/Michelle Kwan showdown, so the pressure was off her. She just had to show that she could do what she'd been trained by so many to do.

At the Nationals in Philadelphia, Nicole was ready to skate. The foregone conclusion was that the USFSA committee would send Tara and Michelle to the Olympics, but this year the United States qualified for three slots in the ladies' figure skating competition based on the U.S. sweep of both first and second places in the 1997 Worlds. Who would be that third person to go to Nagano, Japan? It looked like it would be either Tonia Kwiatkowski or Nicole.

Campbell Soup bet on Nicole, hiring her, Tara, and Michelle to film a TV commercial that aired during the Nationals. They printed soup can labels featuring the three before the final scores had been tallied.

After the short program, executives at Campbell Soup may have had serious doubts about their decision. Michelle skated the performance of her life, and seven of the nine judges awarded her perfect scores of 6.0 for presentation. Nicole skated very well and landed in second after the short program. Tara Lipinski fell on a triple flip and fell to fourth place behind Tonia Kwiatkowski.

Tara Lipinski then skated a flawless long program, which counted two-thirds of the final score, and finished with the silver medal. Nicole left out two of her combination jumps, but skated beautifully and earned a standing ovation from the crowd and the bronze medal. Michelle Kwan exceeded her short program by earning perfect 6.0s for presentation from eight of the nine judges, the highest score ever for a ladies' figure skater. Tonia tumbled to fourth place.

Nicole was thrilled with her third-place finish and a spot on the Olympic team. "It was the kind of performance that I had been hoping for. It was something I had been dreaming of my whole life." She was on top again, but as she observed after Nationals, "My whole life has been an emotional roller coaster."

Talk now in skating circles, around kitchen tables, and around office water coolers was of a sweep at the Olympics.

"We can be 1–2–3," said Nicole's coach, Christa Fassi. "I really think we have the Dream Team for these Olympics."

Michelle's coach, Frank Carroll, agreed because the three skaters presented three different styles. "Nicole looks like a movie star. Michelle has uniquely wonderful artistry. Tara is a wonderful young jumper, technically very strong and consistent."

The three skaters were profiled in various magazines as the hope of the nation for the Olympics. Their lifestyles were studied and comparisons drawn between Michelle's and Tara's dedication and Nicole's erratic practice schedule and her occasional splurges on hamburgers and Mexican food.

But Nicole took her training seriously and practiced the required jumps for the Olympics. Recovering from a hip injury and bronchitis, she was the last of the dream team to arrive in Nagano, Japan. She suffered from jet lag when she took the ice for her first practice session with her teammates.

"I'm a little tired. My legs still feel like they're back home. They're coming over on the next flight," Nicole said with a husky laugh. She fell several times during warmups, but when her time came to practice her short program, she was fine.

On the day of the short program, Nicole arrived at White Ring in Nagano 35 minutes before her group's practice time. Her warmup did not go well, and her routine was even worse. She skated to Herb Alpert's "Zorba the Greek," and although her beginning moves fit the lively music, she fell on her first jump, a triple Lutz combination, which carried a mandatory point reduction. Shaken, she doubled a triple toe loop and stepped out of her double Axel. Her spiral combinations were, as always, a pleasure to watch.

"This is not what you want your Olympics to be," TV commentator and former Olympic gold medalist Scott Hamilton said. "She's an incredible performer. When she's on, she lights up the building like nobody else."

A medal cannot be won by a strong short program, but it can be lost by a bad one. Nicole knew she was out of medal contention when she sat in kiss and cry and waited for marks, which ranged from 4.2 to 4.7 for technical merit, and from 5.0 to 5.5 for artistic presentation. She shed tears of sadness and disappointment and was too devastated to give an on-camera interview.

Michelle Kwan won the short program with Tara Lipinski a close second. Nicole ranked 17th.

At the long program, Nicole was more relaxed, but she did not skate up to her potential. Music from Von Weber's "Invitation to the Dance," Chopin's "Liebestraum," and Verdi's "Victory March" offered tempo variations, but those pesky jumps were her downfall. She doubled her triple Lutz, put her hand on the ice to maintain balance on a triple flip, stepped out of the double Axel, and fell on the triple Lutz and triple Salchow.

In kiss and cry this time, there were no tears, but a relieved, smiling Nicole. When her marks were posted, she shrugged and said, "Oh, well."

After a disappointing short program at White Ring arena in Nagano, Japan, Nicole is hugged by her new coach, Christa Fassi, wife of the late Carlo Fassi.

Later she teased reporters, "Write something nice please, and no pictures of falls.

"It was tough after the short. I really just wanted to give up and go home. I had a lot of people supporting me and telling me, 'It's all right, just go out there and go for it.'

"Hopefully, people will remember me for how hard I tried," she said, "not how I did."

Nicole's dream of Olympic glory had ended, but Tara Lipinski skated the most difficult program of the evening and narrowly beat Michelle Kwan for the gold medal, becoming the youngest figure skating gold medalist. Nicole was 17th.

The weeks between the Olympics and Worlds were full of unexpected events. Nicole changed coaches yet again. She didn't like training at Lake Arrowhead alongside Michelle Kwan, so she practiced at the SkateNation rink in Richmond, Virginia, with Valentin Nikolayev.

Tara Lipinski, suffering from a glandular infection and fatigue, withdrew from the Worlds competition and would not be defending her title. The USFSA committee tapped Tonia Kwiatkowski for Tara's spot.

Then Nicole fell hard on a triple Lutz during practice. She reaggravated a left hip flexor which had given her problems at the Olympics.

"I am very disappointed that this injury will prevent me from competing at the World Championships," Nicole said. "Following a difficult Olympic experience, I had hoped to prove something to myself and the American audience. For that reason, this has been an especially difficult decision for me."

At the event in Minneapolis, Michelle won the gold and Tonia finished sixth. Nicole had lived through many disappointments in her life, and she accepted not skating at the Worlds with dignity and confidence that she soon would be skating again.

Nicole looked to her future as a pro. She had already signed on for the 1998 Campbell Soup summer tour, now called Champions on Ice. Dazzling the crowds with her own graceful style of skating without including those triple jumps appealed to her.

Nicole could add her own choreography to her programs and glide and twirl with the grace and allure for which she was known. She could embrace life with her husky laugh and a twinkle in her eye and enjoy skating without the pressure of competition. Nicole Bobek could find the balance that she had been searching for.

CHRONOLOGY

1977   Born to Jana Bobek in Chicago, Illinois on August 23.

1981   Tries ice skating for the first time.

1982   Gets first professional coach and wins first competition.

1987   Moves to Los Angeles, California.

1989   Places second in National novice competition and moves to Colorado Springs, Colorado.

1990   Places fourth in National junior competition.

1991   Moves to Italy for four months, then moves back to Colorado Springs; places fourth in World Junior Championships; advances to senior level competition and places eighth in U.S. National Figure Skating Championships; wins U.S. Olympic Festival; wins Vienna Cup.

1992   Places seventh in U.S. National Figure Skating Championships.

1993   Places fifth in U.S. National Figure Skating Championships.

1994   Places third in U.S. National Figure Skating Championships and 13th in Qualifying Group B at World Figure Skating Championships; trains in Cape Cod, Massachusetts; trains in Detroit, Michigan.

1995   Wins U.S. National Figure Skating Championship; places third in World Figure Skating Championships; tours with Campbell Soup Tour of World Figure Skating Champions; skates with Nutcracker on Ice tour; trains in Las Vegas, Nevada.

1996   Withdraws from U. S. National Figure Skating Championships because of injury; trains in Lake Arrowhead, California; tours with Campbell Soup Tour of World Figure Skating Champions.

1997   Places third in U.S. National Figure Skating Competition; places 13th in World Figure Skating Competition after Coach Carlo Fassi dies; tours with Campbell Soup Tour of World Figure Skating Champions.

1998   Places third in U.S. National Figure Skating Competition; places 17th in Olympic Games in Nagano, Japan; trains in Richmond, Virginia; withdraws from World Figure Skating Competition because of injury; turns professional; tours with Campbell Soup Champions on Ice.

FURTHER READING

Berman, Alice. *Skater's Edge Sourcebook*. Kensington, MD: Skater's Edge, 1998.

Bezic, Sandra. *The Passion to Skate: An Intimate View of Figure Skating*. Atlanta: Turner Publishing, Inc., 1996.

Brennan, Christine. *Edge of Glory: The Inside Story of the Quest for Figure Skating's Olympic Gold Medals*. New York: Scribner, 1998.

——. *Inside Edge: A Revealing Journey into the Secret World of Figure Skating*. New York: Scribner, 1996.

Gutman, Dan. *Ice Skating From Axels to Zambonis*. New York: Viking, 1995.

Petkevich, John Misha. *Sports Illustrated Figure Skating Championship Techniques*. New York: Time, Inc., 1989.

Smith, Beverly. *Figure Skating: A Celebration*. New York: St. Martin's Press, 1994.

Tresniowski, Alex et al. "Triple Threat." *People Weekly*, February 1998, p. 94.

ABOUT THE AUTHOR

Award-winning writer Veda Boyd Jones enjoys the challenge of writing for a variety of readers. Her published works include nine adult novels, three children's historical novels, two children's biographies, a coloring book, and numerous articles and short stories in national magazines. In addition to working at her computer, she teaches writing and speaks at writers' conferences. Mrs. Jones lives in Missouri with her husband, Jimmie, and three sons, Landon, Morgan, and Marshall.

GLOSSARY

AXEL: a jump named for its inventor, Axel Paulsen. The Axel is the only jump launched while skating forward. A skater takes off from the forward outside skate edge and lands on the opposite foot on a back outside edge. A double Axel is the same jump with two and a half mid-air rotations. A triple Axel, achieved for the first time in 1978, requires three and a half mid-air rotations.

CAMEL: a skating spin performed with one leg extended back; the camel is called a flying camel when a skater jumps into the spin.

CROSSOVER: performed when a skater crosses his or her stride; a crossover tends to increase a skater's speed.

DEATH SPIRAL: a pairs figure skating move in which the man pivots and spins the woman in a circle around him with one hand while her arched body spirals down until it is almost parallel to the ice.

FLIP: a jump made by sticking the blade pick into the ice, revolving, and then landing on the back outside edge of the toe-assisting foot; the triple flip is the same jump with three revolutions.

FOOTWORK: any series of turns, steps, hops, and crossovers done at high speed.

LIFTS: pairs moves in which the man holds the woman up in a ballet-like position over his head; variations on lifts include the star lift, in which the woman holds both her arms in the air, and the one-armed lift, in which the man supports the woman with only one arm.

LOOP: a jump in which the skater takes off and lands on the same back outside edge.

LUTZ: a jump named for its creator, Alois Lutz. For the Lutz, a skater takes off on a back outside edge, revolves, and then lands on a back outside edge. When a skater revolves three times in the air, the jump is called a triple Lutz.

SALCHOW: a jump named after Swedish skater Ulrich Salchow. For the Salchow, a skater makes a long glide backward and then takes off on the outside edge of one skate, with a boost from the toe of the opposite skate. After revolving, the skater lands on the outside edge of the boosting skate. A double Salchow has two rotations; a triple Salchow requires three full rotations while in the air.

SPIN: a skater performs a spin by rotating from one fixed point; when skaters spin, they move so fast their image becomes blurred.

SIT SPIN: a spin in which the skater crouches down, balanced on one leg while the other extends; often a skater will pull up out of a sit spin to a standing spin position.

SPREAD-EAGLE: a move in which a skater glides on two feet, with the lead foot on a forward edge and the trail foot on the same edge, only backward.

TOE LOOP: a jump launched off the toe pick of the free foot in which a skater completes one rotation and lands on the back outside edge of the same foot. The toe pick can launch the skater to a great height; hence, a double toe loop has two mid-air rotations, and a triple toe loop has three.

THROWS: pairs moves in which the man throws the woman into the air, where she spins two or three times before landing on one foot.

INDEX

Picture Credits: AP/Wide World Photos: pp. 2, 6, 8, 10, 16, 19, 20, 26, 28, 32, 35, 40, 42, 43, 46, 51, 52, 54, 57, 60; New York Public Library: pp. 13, 14, 22, 24, 36